HOW MACHINES WORK

TRUCKS

TERRY JENNINGS

FRANKLIN WATTS
LONDON • SYDNEY

An Appleseed Editions book

First published in 2008 by Franklin Watts

Franklin Watts
338 Euston Road, London NW1 3BH

Franklin Watts Australia
Level 17/207 Kent St, Sydney, NSW 2000

© 2008 Appleseed Editions

Appleseed Editions Ltd
Well House, Friars Hill, Guestling, East Sussex TN35 4ET

Created by Q2AMedia
Series Editor: Paul Manning
Book Editor: Katie Dicker
Senior Art Director: Ashita Murgai
Designer: Harleen Mehta, Shilpi Sarkar
Picture Researcher: Amit Tigga

ISBN 978 0 7496 8076 3

Dewey classification: 629.224

All words in **bold** can be found in Glossary on pages 30–31.

Website information is correct at time of going to press. However, the publishers cannot
accept liability for any information or links found on third-party websites.

A CIP catalogue for this book is available from the British Library.

Picture credits
t=top b=bottom c=centre l=left r=right m=middle
Cover images: ©copyright AB Volvo 2008

Scania: 4, John Deere: 5t, Shutterstock: 5b, Freightliner Truck: 6, Scania: 7, Scania: 9b, Volvo: 10, 11b, 12, 13t, 13b,
Studio 3 Inc.: 14, Volvo: 15, Scania: 16, Volvo: 17t, 17b, Scania: 18, Mark Boulton/ Alamy: 19t, DaimlerChrysler: 19bl, 19br,
Stefan Sollfors/ Alamy: 20t, DaimlerChrysler: 20b, Benoit Beauregard/ Istockphoto: 21, Scania: 22-23,
Joy Brown/ Shutterstock: 24t, Regis Duvignau/ Reuters/ Corbis: 24b, Tony Tremblay/ Istockphoto: 25,
Freightliner Truck: 26, Volvo: 27tr, DAF test track: 27bl, DaimlerChrysler: 28–29

Q2AMedia Art Bank: 8, 9t, 11t

Printed in Hong Kong

Franklin Watts is a division of Hachette Children's Books

CONTENTS

TYPES OF TRUCK

A truck's job is to carry heavy loads. There are many different trucks, from petrol tankers to street sweepers. The largest trucks are simply massive!

A truck has a front section that contains the engine and the **cab** where the driver sits. The back section of a truck is for carrying. Some giant trucks have as many as 28 wheels to spread the weight of their huge loads.

▼ Heavy trucks drive long distances day and night to bring us the goods we need

The powerful engine of this long-distance truck can pull loads of up to 60 tonnes

ARTICULATED TRUCKS

The largest trucks come in two parts. The front part, containing the engine and cab, is called a **tractor unit**. The load-carrying part is called a **trailer**. These **articulated trucks** can bend round corners. Trucks that cannot bend are called **rigid trucks**.

▲ This dump truck's chunky tyres provide good grip for hauling heavy loads over rough ground

▼ The trucks that carry goods across Australia are so long they are called **road trains**

Tractor unit

Bull-bar
Prevents damage to engine from stray animals

Trailer

ROAD TRAIN

ENGINE POWER

Trucks that carry heavy loads need powerful engines. Diesel engines used to be noisy and smelly, but today they are quieter, cleaner and more efficient.

Diesel engines work in a similar way to petrol engines, but they burn oil instead of petrol and they do not need spark plugs. In newer engines, **fuel** injectors control the amount of fuel pumped into the **cylinders**. This means that the fuel burns efficiently with less pollution.

▼ This Freightliner truck is powered by a six-cylinder diesel engine like the one shown opposite

FREIGHTLINER CASCADIA	
Specification	
Body Type:	Articulated
Engine:	15.2 l, 6-cylinder
Power:	410 kw (550 hp)
Cab:	Raised-roof sleeper

DID YOU KNOW?
Engine power is usually measured in **horsepower (hp)**. A small family car produces 80 to 150 hp. A large truck diesel engine can produce 3,500 hp!

A TRUCK DIESEL ENGINE

▼ A diesel engine uses a process called compression ignition. Fuel is injected after the air is compressed in the cylinder. This causes the fuel to ignite without the need for spark plugs

Fuel injection system
Pumps diesel fuel into engine cylinders

Fan
Cools engine

Belts
Drive pumps which circulate oil and water

Driveshaft
Transfers power to wheels via gearbox

THE DIESEL ENGINE CYCLE

In a petrol engine, fuel and air are squeezed together and ignited by a spark plug. In a diesel engine, fuel is injected after the air in the cylinder has been squeezed. Because the air becomes very hot when it is squeezed, the fuel ignites without the need for a spark plug.

Inlet valve Opens to let in air

Piston

Cylinder

Fuel Ignites with heat of cylinder

Outlet valve Opens to let out hot waste gases

① SUCK

The piston moves down. The inlet valve opens. Air is drawn into the cylinder

② SQUEEZE

The inlet valve closes. The piston moves up, squashing the air until it is very hot

③ BANG

Diesel oil is squirted into the cylinder. The oil burns without the need for a spark. The piston is pushed back down

④ BLOW

The outlet valve opens. The piston rises and hot waste gases are pushed out of the cylinder

DID YOU KNOW?
During the 'Squeeze' stage of a diesel engine cycle, the air inside the cylinder reaches a temperature of 900°C!

THE TURBOCHARGER

Most modern truck engines are fitted with a **turbocharger**. The **exhaust** gases are used to drive a turbine wheel, which pushes more air into the engine. More air means the diesel burns faster, greatly increasing engine power.

▶ Inside the turbocharger, exhaust gases drive a turbine, which is linked to a compressor unit. The compressor sucks in extra air and forces it into the engine cylinders

▶ All trucks need regular servicing and maintenance. Most larger trucks have a cab that tilts forwards so that the engine can be reached more easily

(1) Exhaust gases from engine drive turbine

(2) Turbine drives compressor

(3) Compressor sucks in fresh air and forces it into engine

Turbine and compressor mounted on shared **axle**

DID YOU KNOW?
Diesel engines burn fuel more efficiently than petrol engines. Even so, a large diesel truck may only travel just over 1.5 km to 1 litre of fuel

HOW A TRUCK IS BUILT

Most trucks are built on a frame, or chassis, which looks like a giant ladder. The engine, cab, axles, brakes and other parts are fixed onto this frame.

Deflector
Smoothes the flow
of air over the trailer

VOLVO FL

Specification	
Body Type:	Rigid
Engine:	7 l, 6-cylinder turbo-diesel
Power:	208 kw (280 hp)
Gearbox	6-speed automatic

Driveshaft
Transmits power
from gearbox to
rear axle

▲ Most chassis frames are made of very strong steel or aluminium, which is lighter

Fuel tank
One on each side to
store diesel oil

**Tubeless
radial tyres**
Reinforced with
steel, grip road in
wet conditions

Disc brakes
Worked by compressed air

Brake pads
Grip disc when brake pedal is pressed

Compressed air
Operates piston

DISC BRAKES

Most trucks today are fitted with electronically controlled brakes (EBS). As soon as the driver presses the brake pedal, pads are squeezed against steel discs fitted to the wheels of the truck. The **friction** makes the discs slow down and brings the truck to a stop.

Piston
Squeezes brake pads together

Disc
Spins with wheel of truck

Tyre

Ladder
Gives access to roof of cab

Wires and tubes
Carry power for lights and brakes

'Fifth wheel'
Metal disc on which trailer swivels

Fuel tanks

▶ When a trailer is attached to the tractor unit, wires and tubes are needed to carry electricity and air to the rear lights and brakes

FROM ENGINE TO WHEELS

The transmission system carries the engine's power to the wheels. It includes the **gears**, the clutch, the driveshaft and the **differential**. Trucks need gears so that the engine can turn the wheels at different speeds. The gears are toothed wheels of different sizes. The clutch smoothly links and unlinks the engine to the wheels as the driver changes gear. It also lets the engine keep running when the truck is not moving.

Trucks may have 16 or more gears. As the driver presses or releases the accelerator pedal, the **automatic transmission** chooses the best gear for the speed and road conditions

▼ The gearbox links the engine to the driveshaft and allows the engine to drive the wheels at different speeds

Input shaft
Receives power from the engine

Gear wheel
Turns larger and smaller gear wheels

Output shaft
Transfers power to the axle and wheels

▼ This truck's differential allows its wheels to turn at different speeds as it goes round corners

THE DIFFERENTIAL

When the truck is travelling in a straight line, the engine drives all the wheels at the same speed. When the truck goes round a bend, the wheels on the outside of the bend have to turn faster to keep up. The differential is a set of gears that lets the outer wheels turn faster to keep up with the turning inner wheels.

▶ The gear wheels of the differential are inside a truck's rear axle

Differential
Allows wheels to turn at different speeds when truck goes round corners

Driveshaft
Transfers engine power to wheels

Rear axle

IN THE CAB

For the driver, one of the most important parts of the truck is the cab. This is where he or she spends most of the day – and sometimes the night, too.

The cab of a long-haul truck is a sitting room, bedroom, kitchen and office all rolled into one. There is room to stand, sit, walk around and stretch out. As well as the bed, there may be a sink, fridge, microwave and television.

The cab of a modern long-haul truck has a microwave, a fridge and a bed where the driver can rest, sleep or watch television

STYLING

The inside of a modern truck cab is as comfortable as a luxury car. The seats are fully adjustable for leg-room, and the floor is carpeted. There is tinted glass in the windscreen, to filter out the glare of the sun, and electric windows. Sound insulation reduces the noise of the engine so the driver can listen to music or take calls on the hands-free cab telephone.

▼ The smooth curves of this truck allow air to flow past and help the engine to work more efficiently

VOLVO FH1L

Specification
Engine: 16 l, 6-cylinder
Power: 492 kw (660 hp)
Cab   Sleeper

Large tinted windscreen
Gives a clear view of the road ahead

'Fifth wheel'
Where trailer is attached and swivels

Radiator grill
Takes in air to cool engine

STEERING

Almost all trucks steer by their front wheels. These wheels are connected by a series of levers and a steering column to a steering wheel inside the cab. Before the days of power-assisted steering, driving a truck used to be very hard work. Now only small, light movements are needed to steer the biggest vehicles.

DID YOU KNOW?
Some trucks are fitted with a device which prevents the vehicle being driven if there are traces of alcohol on the driver's breath

Switches
Control lights and air-conditioning

Air vents
Allow air to enter cab at a comfortable temperature

The controls on the dashboard of this long-haul truck are all designed to be within easy reach of the driver

CONTROLS AND INSTRUMENTS

The truck's wrap-around dashboard gives the driver a good view of the gauges and instruments. As well as a speedometer, milometer and fuel gauge, a truck dashboard may have 50 or more other displays. These let the driver keep an eye on everything from fuel economy to journey time, and flash up warnings of any engine or mechanical faults.

Satellite navigation ('Satnav') tracks the driver's position via satellites orbiting the earth. The interactive screen and prerecorded voice tell the driver which route to take to save time and avoid traffic queues.

▼ In-cab radio keeps drivers entertained and gives them important travel information on long journeys

Satellite navigation (see above)

Radio and CD player

TRUCKS AT WORK

Shops, petrol stations and factories all rely on trucks to deliver their supplies. Many trucks are specially designed for the loads they carry.

Trucks that carry meat, fish, poultry, milk and other food products have to be temperature-controlled. A special diesel engine at the front of the truck powers a refrigeration unit to keep the goods fresh while they are on the road.

▼ A petrol tanker sets off from the depot with a cargo of fuel for delivery to petrol stations

DID YOU KNOW?
Drivers in charge of dangerous or **combustible** loads have to be specially trained and must follow strict safety rules

CARRYING LIQUIDS

Tankers that carry liquids often have five or six compartments inside. This means that a petrol tanker can carry a different grade or type of petrol in each of the compartments. It also prevents the liquid sloshing around from one end of the tanker to the other, making the truck difficult to drive.

▼ This 40-tonne tanker can carry up to to 25,000 litres of milk in special temperature-controlled compartments

▲ This truck is used to re-stock aircraft with pre-packed in-flight meals. The insulated box body at the rear of the truck can be raised up to 8 m to reach the body of the aircraft

STREET CLEANING

Trucks that carry away our rubbish, sweep our streets and empty drains need to have special tools for the job. Modern refuse collection trucks have automatic transmission so the truck can move from house to house without the driver needing to change gear. Inside the truck, the rubbish is crushed and squeezed so it takes up less space.

▼ This street cleaner has rotating brushes to sweep up dirt, leaves and litter. A vacuum pipe sucks the rubbish into the container at the back of the truck

◀ This dust cart has mechanical arms for lifting and emptying plastic bins

Vacuum pipe
Sucks up dirt

Rotating brushes
Sweep gutters

SNOW CLEARING

When there is heavy snow in winter, snow ploughs and snow blowers clear the roads so that traffic can keep moving. The blade on the front of a snow plough pushes the snow to the side of the road. A snow blower pushes the snow upwards with a spinning drum. The snow is then blown out to the side of the road.

▼ Snow ploughs need powerful engines to push aside heavy piles of snow and ice

Warning light
Tells other road users to slow down and keep clear

DID YOU KNOW?
The first snow ploughs were large wooden wedges pulled by teams of horses

Steel blade
Angled to push snow to side of road

Powerful headlights
To see through snow or fog

GRAB, LIFT AND LOAD!

Trucks that carry heavy loads need to be fitted with special tools. Some have powerful mechanical arms for grabbing, lifting and loading.

▼ These massive logs can be loaded easily by the driver using a truck-mounted **hydraulic grab**

Hydraulic arm
Operates grab and folds away when not in use

Grab
Works like giant hand

SCANIA R470 6X4 TIMBER TRANSPORT

Specification

Engine:	12 litre, 6 cylinder
Power:	350 kw (470 hp)
Cab:	Extended day cab

SELF-LOADERS

Trucks that deliver bricks, concrete blocks or other heavy materials to building sites often use self-loading cranes. Dump trucks that collect soil, rocks or other loose materials use a built-in grab, or shovel. Trucks that carry metal shipping containers often have their own hydraulic 'swing-lift' gear.

▼ The side-lifting equipment on this truck can lift weights of up to 30 tonnes

SCANIA R420

Specification
Engine: 12 l, 6 cylinder
Power: 313 kw (420 hp)
Cab: Day or sleeper

Telescopic crane
Folds away when not in use

Driver
Operates crane by remote-control handset

Hydraulic stabilizer
Takes weight off wheels and steadies truck

▶ Car transporters are very expensive trucks. A computer inside the cab works out the best loading order for the cars

HAULAGE TRUCKS

Heavy haulage trucks are among the biggest and most powerful vehicles on the road. They are used to move anything from giant wind turbines to the bodies of aircraft or railway locomotives. The trailer may have a large number of small wheels, and be pulled by three or four tractor units.

▼ This truck has been loaded with part of an Airbus A380 – the biggest aircraft ever built. It will drive the component 240 km to a factory for assembly. A powerful tractor unit drags a large trailer to move this colossal load

SPECIAL LOADS

Logging trucks are specially built to carry huge tree trunks. Special trailers with upright metal rods at the side called bolsters are used to carry the logs, which are held in place with chains. Some of the largest logging trucks can pull three or more trailers, each carrying around 50 tonnes.

▼ This truck is specially built for carrying timber. Bolsters at the sides hold the logs firmly in place during transit

Bolsters

FUTURE TRUCKS

Truck design is changing fast. As fuel costs rise, new ways are being found to make engines more efficient and to improve speed, comfort and reliability.

For many years, truck engines have run on petrol or diesel. But as supplies of oil run low, manufacturers are looking at other sources of energy. They are also exploring ways to make trucks cleaner and more fuel-efficient.

▼ Reducing wind-resistance cuts the amount of fuel a truck uses. In this **wind tunnel** test, special fog is blown at a model truck to see how easily air flows around it

The **streamlined** shape of this truck means that its engine does not have to push so hard against the wind. This reduces the amount of fuel it uses

NEW ENGINES, NEW FUELS

New types of **biodiesel** trucks use fuels made from plants, such as oilseed rape and sunflowers. Some trucks run on natural gas and others use fuels made from alcohol or even gases produced by rotting plants. All these fuels are cheaper and cleaner to use than petrol or diesel.

TRUCK TESTING

New types of truck are tested for many months before they are allowed on public roads. As well as wind tunnel tests, trucks are tested in the laboratory and on special outdoor tracks to make sure they are fit for the road.

▲ A laboratory technician tests a new truck engine to make sure it runs cleanly and quietly

◀ This truck is being driven on a special track to test its brakes and **suspension**

DRIVERLESS TRUCKS

An exciting development in truck design is the 'electronic drawbar'. The drawbar allows a convoy of up to five trucks to be linked electronically. The trucks that follow automatically copy everything done by the lead truck, including its steering, acceleration and braking. The trucks are kept a safe distance apart, varying between 6 and 15 m, depending on how fast they are travelling.

DID YOU KNOW?
When two trucks use an electronic drawbar, the second truck uses up to 20% less fuel than the first, depending on speed

▼ These two trucks have only one driver! Everything the front truck does is copied electronically by the truck behind

IMPROVED FEATURES

The latest designs for trucks are much more curvy and streamlined. Huge windscreens can be darkened in bright sunlight. Instead of rear-view mirrors, cameras send images of what is behind the truck to a monitor in the driver's cab. **Radar** warns if other vehicles get too close.

▼ These design sketches show plans for a new truck

Driver's seat
In raised central position for best view of road

Streamlined shape
Saves fuel and money

Spacious living area
Allows more room for driver to rest and relax

Wrap-around windscreen
For clear, all-round view

Cameras
Instead of wing mirrors

Side opening
Allows truck to be loaded more easily

◀ New designs make trucks easier to drive, steer and load and less costly to run

GLOSSARY

Articulated truck
A truck with a separate tractor unit pulling a trailer. An articulated truck can bend as it goes round corners

Automatic transmission
A gearbox that automatically changes gear, depending on the speed of the vehicle

Axle A metal rod on which the wheels of a truck are mounted

Biodiesel A fuel made from natural sources such as vegetable oil or animal fat, which can be used in a diesel engine

Cab The front part of a truck where the driver sits

Combustible
Able to burn

Cylinder The part of an engine where the fuel is burned

Diesel engine A type of engine that burns diesel oil

Differential A set of gears that lets the wheels turn at different speeds when a truck turns a corner

Exhaust Waste gases from the engine that pass out through the exhaust pipe, or are used in a turbocharger

'Fifth wheel' A metal device that allows the trailer to swivel on the tractor unit

Friction A rubbing force that tries to stop two objects moving against each other

Fuel The substance burned in an engine to provide power

Gear A set of toothed wheels that transmit power from the engine to the wheels of a truck

Horsepower (hp) A unit used to measure the power of an engine

Hydraulic grab
A type of pincer, powered by the force of a liquid squeezed inside a cylinder

Radar A device that sends out and receives radio waves to measure how close an object is

Rigid truck A truck where the cab and engine and the load section do not come apart

Road train A very long truck with a tractor unit pulling at least three trailers

Streamlined Shaped to move through air easily. A streamlined truck has a smooth, gently curved shape

Suspension A system of springs that link the truck's frame to the wheels to give a smooth ride

Tractor unit The front part of an articulated truck containing the driver's cab, engine and driving wheels

Trailer A load carrier that hooks onto the tractor unit to form an articulated truck

Turbocharger A device that uses waste gases to increase the amount of fuel burned in an engine, to make it more powerful

Wind tunnel Equipment for studying how easily air flows around a truck as it drives along

INDEX

Websites

http://www.roadway.com/kids/trucks.html
An educational site with facts, activities and an interactive game

http://www.volvo.com/trucks/na/en-ca/products/loading_ramp/kids_corner/
Build a truck, take a drive and try out some puzzles and games

http://auto.howstuffworks.com/diesel.htm
An introduction to how a diesel engine works